The Georgians

Usborne Quicklinks

The Usborne Quicklinks website is packed with thousands of links to all the best websites on the internet. The websites include information, video clips, sounds, games and animations that support and enhance the information in Usborne internet-linked books.

To visit the recommended websites for this book, go to the Usborne Quicklinks website at **www.usborne.com/quicklinks** and enter the keywords **The Georgians**.

When using the internet please follow the internet safety guidelines displayed on the Usborne Quicklinks website. The recommended websites in Usborne Quicklinks are regularly reviewed and updated, but Usborne Publishing Ltd. is not responsible for the content or availability of any website other than its own. We recommend that children are supervised while using the internet.

USBORNE HISTORY OF BRITAIN

The Georgians

Ruth Brocklehurst & Hazel Maskell

Illustrated by
Ian McNee & Lynn Stone

Designed by
Anna Gould, Tom Lalonde & Stephen Moncrieff

Edited by Jane Chisholm

Consultant: Prof. Stephen Conway,
University College, London

Contents

A time of revolutions

In 1714, Queen Anne, the last Stuart monarch, died and the throne passed to her heir, George Elector of Hanover. Over the next 100 years or so, the country was ruled by four Hanoverian kings named George. So this period is often known as the Georgian age.

It was a time in which Britain became the world's leading naval power, laying the foundations of an empire in India, but losing another in America. The Georgians saw great advances in farming and the beginning of the Industrial Revolution. Meanwhile, political revolutions overseas rocked the old order, and led to social and political changes in Britain too.

A German king

Geeorge I was 54 years old when he first stepped on British soil, in 1714, to be crowned the nation's King. He was the ruler of the German state of Hanover, spoke only broken English and had little interest in British affairs. Many British people disliked the idea of being ruled by a foreigner, but as the great grandson of James I, and Queen Anne's closest Protestant relative, he was the best choice.

The Hanoverian had few kingly qualities to win the respect of his new subjects. It was said that his main interests were food, horses and women. He had a cruel streak too. Twenty years earlier, he had divorced his wife for having an affair. He forbade her from seeing their children ever again, and had her locked in a castle for the rest of her life. His son, the future George II, was nine years old at the time. He never forgave his father, and the pair argued constantly.

A German court

The new King arrived in London with a host of German nobles, a German composer named Handel, and two German-speaking Turkish servants.

He also brought his two German mistresses with him. One was short and fat, and the other was tall and skinny.

Deeply unpopular, the women were nicknamed the 'Elephant' and the 'Maypole' by the British public.

In this painting Handel (in red) is presenting his musicians to the King as they are rowed along the Thames. They are playing his composition *Water Music*.

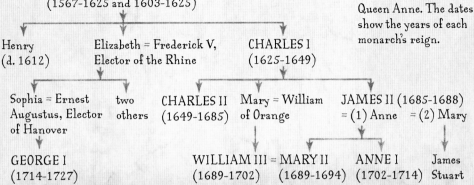

Kings and queens

JAMES VI of Scotland and I of England
(1567-1625 and 1603-1625)

Henry
(d. 1612)

Elizabeth = Frederick V,
Elector of the Rhine

CHARLES I
(1625-1649)

Sophia = Ernest
Augustus, Elector
of Hanover

two
others

CHARLES II
(1649-1685)

Mary = William
of Orange

JAMES II (1685-1688)
= (1) Anne   = (2) Mary

GEORGE I
(1714-1727)

WILLIAM III = MARY II
(1689-1702)   (1689-1694)

ANNE I
(1702-1714)

James
Stuart

This family tree shows
how George I and James
Stuart were related to
Queen Anne. The dates
show the years of each
monarch's reign.

A Scottish contender

There was another reason why not everyone in Britain
warmed to their new King. Many believed that Queen
Anne's half-brother, James Stuart, was the rightful heir.
Parliament had opposed his claim to the throne
because he was a Catholic. But some of his supporters
– known as Jacobites – were prepared to fight to put
the Stuart family back on the throne.

Matters came to a head after George I sacked a
leading politician, a Scotsman named John Erskine,
the Earl of Mar. In retaliation, Mar raised an army of
Jacobites in the Scottish Highlands. In November 1715,
Mar's army fought government forces at Sheriffmuir,
near Stirling. But neither side won a clear victory.

It was only then that James arrived in Scotland from
France, where he was in exile. But he came without an
army, and when the Dutch sent forces to join the
Hanoverians, the Jacobite rebellion collapsed. To
prevent another rising, George I had five Jacobite
leaders beheaded and posted large numbers of
troops in Scotland. James fled back into exile, and
never again posed a real threat to King George.

Jacobite dress

Being a Jacobite in
Georgian Britain was
almost like being a
member of a secret society.

Many Jacobites wore
a sprig of white
heather, or a white
feather in their
hats, as a
symbol of
their loyalty
to the Stuarts.

A Scottish Jacobite, Lord
Nithsdale, was due to be
beheaded for his part in
the 1715 rising. But he
escaped from the Tower
of London by disguising
himself as a female friend
of his wife's.

This Georgian illustration shows Robert Walpole standing to talk to the ministers of the Cabinet.

Walpole was a skilled and persuasive debater, but he was also known for his lack of tact and his crude manners. The look on the face of the bishop at the far right suggests he disapproves of something Walpole has just said.

A wily Whig

With the Jacobite threat dealt with for the time being, George I was free to get on with the business of government. But he took little interest in British affairs and, because of his poor English, he seldom met with his ministers. Instead, he left the Cabinet – a council of top ministers – to run the country, while he spent as much time as he could in Hanover.

Divided rule

There were two main political parties in Georgian Britain: the Whigs and the Tories. But a number of Tories had backed the Jacobites, and George made it clear that he would not allow them to take power. In fact, the Whigs would dominate Parliament for the rest of the 18th century. But without a real opposition, the Whigs began to fight among themselves. They split into two main groups, one behind the King, and the other behind his most bitter rival – his son, George.

Boom and bust

Then, in 1720, the government was nearly toppled by a financial crisis. A trading venture, called the South Sea Company, had been selling shares on the promise of vast profits. Thousands of people – from small investors to politicians and even the King – rushed to buy the shares, which immediately shot up in value. This frenzy became known as the South Sea Bubble – and in 1720 it burst. The company wasn't making the profits it had hoped for, the value of its shares crashed, and many investors were bankrupted.

The first Prime Minster

A shrewd, ambitious Whig named Robert Walpole, emerged to take charge of the situation. He rescued the government from collapse and stabilized the country's finances. With many of his opponents ruined when the South Sea Bubble burst, Walpole became the most powerful minister in Parliament. In effect, Walpole was Britain's first Prime Minister, although at that time the title was only used as a term of abuse.

In 1727, George I died in Hanover. He was little mourned in Britain, least of all by his son, who became George II. Walpole tried to keep taxes low by avoiding costly wars, but the new King was itching for glory on the battlefield.

In 1739, war broke out, first against Spain, then France. It was the end for Walpole. He resigned in February 1742 after 21 years in power – still the longest term of any British prime minister.

Number 10

In 1735 George II gave the house at 10 Downing Street to Robert Walpole to live and work in.

It is still the official residence of the Prime Minister today.

This is a detail from a painting of George II leading his troops against the French at the Battle of Dettingen. He was the last British king ever to go into battle.

This photograph shows the grand, Roman-style entrance to Stowe House, which was designed by the architect Robert Adam.

On tour

During the 18th century, it became customary for the young men (and sometimes their sisters) of wealthy families to go on a 'grand tour' of Europe.

Similar to a gap year, this was a long trip that took young adventurers to key cities and monuments, particularly in France and Italy, to learn about European culture.

Many returned home laden with works of art they had collected during their travels.

Landed gentry

With his great power, Robert Walpole was able to acquire a great fortune. And he spent much of it building Houghton Hall, a grand house on the site of his ancestral home in Norfolk. In the first half of the 18th century, much of the British countryside was in the hands of only a few hundred wealthy families – the 'landed gentry' – who dominated politics and business, and wanted their country homes to reflect their wealth, power and good taste.

Classical elegance

Houghton Hall was just one of many large 'stately homes' built, or rebuilt, by Georgian landowners. It was among the first to be designed in an elegant style that became fashionable in the 1730s, known as 'Palladian' architecture. Inspired by the ancient Roman temples and villas of Italy, this style used tall columns, geometric proportions and clean lines to create a commanding impression on the surrounding landscape.

10

Power houses

These great buildings were more than family homes. Some became places of learning, playing host to artists and poets. One of the most impressive stately homes was Stowe, in Buckinghamshire, which belonged to a leading Whig named Viscount Cobham. It became the headquarters for 'Cobham's Cubs' – a group of Whigs set up in opposition to Walpole.

A capable gardener

The grounds at Stowe were landscaped by a 26-year-old named Lancelot 'Capability' Brown, who went on to become the most sought after landscape gardener of the day. He earned his nickname because he could always see the "capability for improvement" in any garden.

Under his influence, it became fashionable to create country parks with wide, sweeping lawns, informal flower beds, lakes and striking features, such as statues, fake Roman ruins and temples. At Stowe, Cobham had more than 30 monuments and 50 statues installed.

Funny walls

Many stately homes were surrounded by a sunken wall known as a ha-ha. This kept out wild animals and trespassers, without interrupting the views of the countryside from the house.

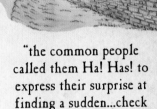

"the common people called them Ha! Has! to express their surprise at finding a sudden...check to their walk."

Robert Walpole's son Horace attempts to explain where the term 'Ha-Ha' came from.

Robert Adam

One of the most influential Georgian architects working in the Palladian style was a Scotsman named Robert Adam, whose portrait is shown here.

He designed many stately homes and public buildings, including Stowe, parts of the University of Edinburgh, and Kenwood House, in London.

Adam sometimes designed interiors too. This is one of his drawings for a reading room in a town house.

Sleazy living

Its stately homes may have looked genteel, but Britain in the 1720s and 30s was a violent, crime-ridden place. Extreme poverty and hunger drove some people to petty crime, simply to survive. Meanwhile, a number of politicians and public officials were involved in corruption scandals, as they abused their positions to gain even more wealth and power. Walpole himself was not above using bribery to get what he wanted.

Writers, such as Jonathan Swift, John Gay and Alexander Pope, and artists including William Hogarth and Thomas Rowlandson, used satire in their works to criticize the immorality they saw at all levels of society.

Theatrical satire

John Gay's play *The Beggar's Opera* was a huge box office hit in 1728. It included characters that satirized Robert Walpole and Jonathan Wild.

In this picture by a Georgian cartoonist Thomas Rowlandson, an excited mob is watching as two cocks fight to the death. Fights such as this were extremely bloody, as the birds were often fitted with razor-sharp spurs around their legs.

Social vices

Violent sports such as bear baiting, cock fighting and bare-knuckle boxing were all hugely popular, and spectators would add to the thrill of the fight by placing bets on the results. Coffee houses, inns and clubs provided ample opportunities for gambling at cards or betting on public events, births and deaths.

Drunk and disorderly

This picture is *Gin Lane*, by William Hogarth. It shows a destitute mother who is so drunk on gin that she has dropped her baby.

Cheap, strong gin became a popular drink in the early 18th century, and was wrecking people's lives. Religious leaders and politicians also feared that it was causing laziness and crime among the working classes.

Walpole's government tried to clamp down on the gin trade. But it backed down in 1743, after mobs began shouting "No gin, no King!"

But the gin problem got worse and worse, as the British were drinking 8 million gallons a year. So, in 1751, the Gin Act was brought in to limit the production and consumption of gin.

Organized crime

Georgian Britain was a pretty lawless place. Gangs of poachers roamed country estates and royal parks, hunting for animals to feed their families or to sell. Highwaymen, like Dick Turpin, lurked in country roads, robbing mail coaches and passers-by. Pirates raided trade ships, and smugglers secretly imported luxury goods – such as silks, tea and brandy – without paying taxes on them. But crime was worst in towns, where gangs of pickpockets and thieves operated.

There was no national police force, but local magistrates offered rewards to anyone who caught a criminal. A few people, such as Londoner Jonathan Wild, made a living as 'thief takers'. Until he was caught and hanged, he also made money sending out thieves to steal goods, which he then sold back to their unsuspecting owners.

Paying the price

Criminals who were caught faced severe punishments. Even pickpocketing could be punished by hanging.

Jack Shepherd was one of the most infamous petty thieves. He had been arrested several times, and escaped from prison each time before he was finally hanged, aged 22.

His escapades made him a local hero. Some 200,000 Londoners went to his hanging, hoping that he might even escape death.

The Stuarts' last stand

Only 30 years after the earlier Jacobite rising, James Stuart's dashing and charismatic son, Charles Edward Stuart, renewed the campaign to restore the Stuarts to the British throne. Fondly known by his supporters as 'Bonnie Prince Charlie', Charles landed in Scotland in July, 1745, to make his claim.

Bonnie Prince Charlie is often depicted as a handsome and romantic hero, as in this portrait. Here, his clothes are made from tartan cloth.

Rebel rousing

Bonnie Prince Charlie was joined by only a few Scottish clans. The French sent help, but it was too little and too late to make a difference. Even so, he had some success, capturing Edinburgh, and then marching south into England.

By December, the Jacobites had got as far as Derby, but they failed to muster enough support in England to risk advancing to London. King George may not have been very popular, but people had become used to life under the Hanoverians. With government troops hot on their heels, the Jacobite rebels fled back to Scotland, and eventually to the Highlands.

The final battle

On April 16, 1746, the two armies met at the Battle of Culloden Moor in the north of Scotland, near Inverness. Better trained and equipped, the Hanoverian troops outnumbered the Jacobites by around 9,000 to 6,000. The Jacobites were utterly defeated, in a battle that is said to have lasted less than an hour.

A wanted man

Charlie went on the run in the Highlands. The government sent troops to track him down, and even offered a £30,000 reward for his capture. But the Prince managed to avoid arrest, and his supporters took great risks to protect him, offering him food and shelter wherever he went. A woman named Flora MacDonald helped him to reach the Isle of Skye disguised as her maid. From there, a ship picked him up, and he sailed back to France.

In the aftermath, the government dealt harshly with the Jacobites. Around 3,500 were imprisoned, and many of them were transported to penal colonies overseas. Their leaders were charged with treason and executed. It was the Stuarts' last stand, and the last full-scale battle ever to be fought in Britain. Bonnie Prince Charlie died in exile. With his death all hope of restoring the Stuarts to the British throne ended for good.

This is a Georgian artist's impression of the Battle of Culloden, showing the Jacobites being defeated by the government's 'redcoat' troops in red uniforms.

Cracking down on the clans

For nearly 40 years after the Battle of Culloden, the British government banned people from wearing kilts and playing bagpipes. The ban was only lifted once politicians were sure the Jacobite threat was over.

Fat of the land

Just a few years after the Battle of Culloden, the Highlanders were dealt another blow. During the 1760s, Scottish landlords began to evict tenant farmers forcibly from their land, usually to replace them with sheep farming, which was more lucrative. Whole communities were uprooted, in what became known as the Highland Clearances. Many moved to towns in search of work, but many more emigrated to America.

The clearances were only a part of a series of changes to rural life and farming methods throughout Britain during the 18th century. Some historians now refer to these changes as the Agricultural Revolution.

Enclosures

Until the late 1600s, farming had changed little in Britain for hundreds of years. Most families grew their own food on narrow strips of land in big, open fields that belonged to wealthy landowners. They kept a few animals on common land, and some made a little money by spinning yarn, or weaving cloth at home.

But, from around 1750, more and more British landowners decided that they wanted to make their land more productive and to increase their profits. They took over the strips and made large fields enclosed by fences or hedges. Some cleared forests, drained marshes and took over common land, too.

The new enclosed fields were grouped together to make large farms. These were rented out, but at a much higher rate than before, which most farmers could not afford. This meant that many people no longer had anywhere to grow their food, and were forced to leave the villages where their families had lived for generations, to find work elsewhere.

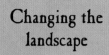

Changing the landscape

This diagram shows an area of farmland made up of open fields, divided into strips. The strips are shown in the same shades as the cottage of the farmer who works on them.

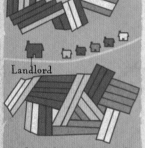

Landlord

Below, the same area of land is divided into two profitable farms, after enclosure.

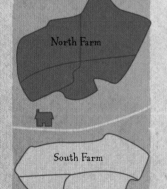

North Farm

South Farm

Modern methods

To make the most of their land, Georgian farmers began trying out new ideas and developing new machines to do some of the hard work for them. One of the most important machines was the seed drill, invented by an English farmer named Jethro Tull. Instead of scattering seeds over the ground by hand, the drill planted seeds carefully in the soil.

Traditionally, many farmers rotated their crops, planting a different crop in each field every year, and regularly leaving each field fallow (unplanted) to rest the soil. But Viscount Townsend learned from Dutch farmers that planting the resting fields with crops like turnips and clover instead, actually enriched the soil, as well as providing food for cattle during the winter.

Fat cows

Some farmers, including Robert Bakewell and Thomas Coke, began using only their best, biggest cattle, sheep and pigs for breeding.

These animals often had big babies, so livestock became significantly larger during the 18th century.

This is a Georgian cartoon, by James Gillray, of a country squire showing off one of his vast bulls.

Trade and empire

Human cargo

Hundreds of slaves were crammed onto each slave ship – the more a ship's captain could carry, the more he would be paid.

Conditions on board were appalling. Slaves were chained up for the entire eight week voyage. More than a third died in transit from disease, thirst and hunger.

This plan made by a slave trader shows how slaves were tightly packed into a ship.

Since Stuart times, British traders had been sailing around the world. They brought tea, textiles, gold and spices from China and India, and tobacco, cotton and sugar from plantations in North America and the Caribbean back to ports at London, Bristol, Liverpool and Glasgow. British manufactured goods, such as woven cloth, guns and iron tools, were then shipped to West Africa in return for slaves, who were transported across the Atlantic to work on the plantations.

This trade grew rapidly, making British owners of merchant ships, factories and plantations incredibly wealthy. By George II's reign, the British had set up many trading colonies around the globe.

Global power struggle

In 1756, a war broke out between Britain and France over colonial territories in India and America. This war was part of what later became known as the Seven Years' War. Fighting also took place in Europe with Britain, Hanover and Prussia on one side, against France, Austria, Russia, Sweden and Spain on the other. Because it was fought across three continents, many historians see this as the first ever global war.

Rivalry in America

By now, the British had many colonies along the east coast of America. But the French, who controlled much of the trade in Canada, built a series of forts along the Great Lakes, the Ohio River and the Mississippi, to try to encircle the British colonies and prevent them from expanding westward. Local skirmishes broke out, and at first the French had the upper hand.

18

Sending in the redcoats

Britain's Secretary of State was William Pitt, a politician who had risen to power as one of Cobham's Cubs. Determined to drive out the French, he built up the nation's army, nicknamed the redcoats, and sent a massive military expedition to America in 1758.

The British troops, along with American soldiers, began in New York and worked their way north. The first French fort they captured was Duquesne, which they renamed Pittsburg. From then on, the French forts fell to the British one by one. In the summer of 1759, they reached the French city of Quebec, in Canada.

Perched on a steep cliff above a river, with French troops on all sides, Quebec seemed impenetrable. But James Wolfe, a talented young general leading the British, had a plan. Under cover of night, he led 5,000 men in rowing boats downriver, where they silently scaled the cliffs to launch a surprise dawn raid on the French. Quebec was taken, and by 1760, the British controlled Montreal and most of Canada, too.

This painting shows the Battle of Quebec in 1759. Both General Wolfe and the French commander were wounded in the battle, and died soon after.

"I believe that I can save the country and that no one else can."

William Pitt believed that the French posed a dangerous threat, not only to Britain's colonies, but to Britain itself.

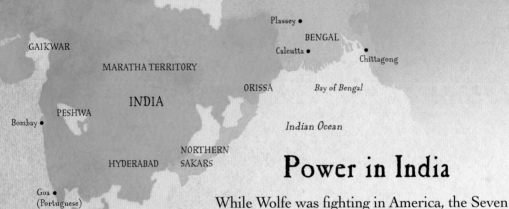

Dehli

Plassey •

BENGAL

Calcutta •

Chittagong

GAIKWAR

MARATHA TERRITORY

ORISSA

INDIA

Bay of Bengal

PESHWA

Bombay •

Indian Ocean

NORTHERN
SAKARS

HYDERABAD

Goa •
(Portuguese)

MYSORE

Arcot • Madras
•
Seringapatam

Mysore • CARNATIC
Pondicherry

Arabian Sea

CEYLON
(now Sri Lanka)

British in India

This map shows the
gradual spread of British
power in India during
the Georgian period.

Land under
British control by:

1767

1805

An Indian
soldier, or
sepoy, in the
British
East India
Company's
army uniform

Power in India

While Wolfe was fighting in America, the Seven
Years' War also spread to India, where the British
East India Company had set up trading posts in
Calcutta, Bombay and Madras. Thousands of
British settlers lived in these bases, governed by
the company and defended by its own army. At
this time, India was divided into many areas
ruled by local princes who often fought each
other. Meanwhile, the French set up bases at
Arcot and Pondicherry.

Now, the British and the French began to take
sides in local wars as they competed for power in
India. The first major British victory came in 1751,
when Robert Clive, a young East India Company clerk,
led a small force of 200 British soldiers and 300 Indians
to seize Arcot.

The Black Hole of Calcutta

In 1756, the ruler, or *Nawab*, of Bengal captured
Calcutta from the British. He took 146 prisoners and
locked them overnight in a small, hot cell, with little
ventilation and no water. Only 23 survived what has
gone down in history as the 'Black Hole of Calcutta'.

20

Gains and losses

Outraged, the British counterattacked. At the Battle of Plassey in 1757, Clive's army defeated the Nawab's much larger forces, who also had French support. This victory gave the British East India Company effective control of Bengal, and weakened the French hold on India. In 1761, the British captured Pondicherry, and two years later the Seven Years' War finally came to an end. The peace treaty that followed gave the British the upper hand in both America and India.

From then on, the British East India Company's prosperity grew steadily, as it gained more territories and privileges through wars and deals with local rulers. Eventually, the British government decided that India was too valuable to be left in the hands of a private company. So in 1784, it took control of all political decisions made in India.

It was Britain's first step on the road to building an empire in India.

This painting by Francis Hayman, shows Robert Clive meeting Mir Jafar, the commander of the army of the Nawab of Bengal.

At this meeting, Clive persuaded Mir Jafar to switch sides, and together they went on to defeat the Nawab of Bengal at the Battle of Plassey.

Textiles and technology

Around the same time that farming methods were improving at home and British trade was growing overseas, manufacturing in Britain began to change too. It was the beginning of what became known as the Industrial Revolution.

Cottage industry

At the start of the 18th century, people lived in the countryside. Britain already had a flourishing cloth industry, and it was this that led the way into the industrial age. Until the 1730s, most textile workers worked at home, spinning thread from wool, flax or imported cotton, and weaving it into cloth using basic spinning wheels and small looms.

But that all changed as new tools and machines were invented that made this work faster and more productive. First came John Kay's 'flying shuttle' which allowed threads to be thrown across the loom, rather than being passed through by hand. Not only was this quicker, but it also meant that weavers could make broader cloth.

These are two 'flying shuttles' designed by John Kay in 1733. Rollers at either end guide the shuttles across the loom.

This painting from the early 19th century shows the cotton mills and houses that were built for the factory workers at New Lanark in Scotland.

Factory life

As the weaving process became faster, hand spinners struggled to keep up with the demand. So, machines were invented that could spin more threads faster. Next, inventors developed new ways to use energy from water wheels to power bigger and better spinning and weaving machines. The new machines were costly to build and too big to use at home, so wealthy businessmen began to build factories to house them.

As other industries expanded in a similar way, factories sprang up around the country, especially in hilly areas in the north of England, where there were plenty of fast-flowing rivers to drive the water wheels. Traditional craftsmen couldn't compete with the new industries, so they were forced to leave home to find work in the factories. These also drew farmers who had become unemployed after enclosures. As towns soon grew around the factories, the old country life began to die out.

But the Industrial Revolution was more than a series of new inventions. The development of banking, increased foreign trade, improved agriculture and a rise in the population all played a part too.

Spinning yarn

Before the 18th century, most fabric in Britain was made from wool. But, as raw cotton from the West Indies and America became more readily available, the demand for cotton cloth grew – until it far outstripped that for wool.

A spinning wheel could only make one reel of thread at a time.

In 1764, James Hargreaves invented the hand-operated 'Spinning Jenny' which could spin 16 threads at a time.

Richard Arkwright took things a step further in 1769 with a water-powered spinning machine. In 1785, Edmund Cartwright made the first water-powered loom, which was later driven by steam.

Highways and waterways

British industry was also helped to grow by enormous improvements in transportation. At the beginning of the Georgian age, many of the nation's roads were no more than dirt tracks, full of potholes that became waterlogged and muddy as soon as it rained. But more and more merchants and manufacturers needed to transport goods around the country, and they were frustrated that the atrocious state of the roads was affecting their businesses. Something had to be done.

Turnpike trusts

Improving the roads would be expensive, so local parishes leased stretches of track to organizations called turnpike trusts. The trusts built thousands of miles of new roads, and repaired and maintained the old ones, sometimes making them straighter too. In return, they collected a fee, or toll, from people who used them. Tolls were collected at gatehouses built at either end of the turnpike roads.

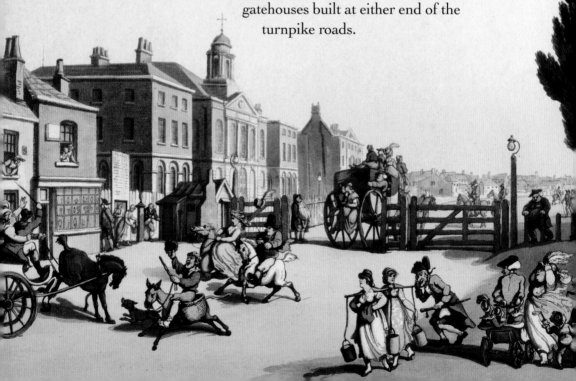

This scene captures the bustling activity at the turnpike on Tottenham Court Road, on the outskirts of London, as people pass through the gate to pay their toll.

Horse power

The Georgians relied so much on horses that there were millions more in 18th century Britain than there are today.

The new road system made travel easier and quicker than ever before. In 1720, it would have taken three days to reach London from Manchester. By 1770, the journey could be completed in a day. And, as the amount of traffic on the roads grew, engineers such as Thomas Telford and Robert Macadam developed methods of building stronger, smoother roads.

Horses drew coaches and carts along the roads...

Heavy goods

But the horses and carts couldn't cope with the increasingly heavy loads of goods and raw materials, such as coal and iron, being transported around the country. Where possible, these goods were taken by barges along rivers; where there wasn't a river, a canal was dug.

...pulled farm machinery...

One of the first Georgian canals was built by an engineer named James Brindley, in 1759. It linked the Earl of Bridgewater's coal mines in Worsley to his factories in Manchester. Over the next 50 years, a vast network of over 6,000km (3,720 miles) of canals was constructed across Britain. Along with the turnpikes – and, later, the railways – the canals transformed the country, and allowed Britain's trade and industry to flourish.

...and towed barges down the canals.

Thousands were also needed for the cavalry.

King and constitution

In 1760 George II died and was succeeded by his 22-year-old grandson, George. Unlike the two kings before him, George III was born and educated in Britain, and was fiercely proud to be British. In fact, he never visited Hanover. He would be King for 60 years – although in the last decade he was too ill to rule for himself – and was held in much affection by his people.

Home life

George III was quiet, shy and deeply religious. His father, Prince Frederick, had died when he was 12, so the main male influence in his childhood was his tutor, his mother's friend John Stuart, the Earl of Bute.

On Bute's advice, George married a German princess, Charlotte of Meklenburg-Strelitz, soon after he became King. It proved a very happy marriage. Unlike his predecessors, George was utterly faithful to his wife, and the couple had fifteen children together. They lived relatively modestly, eating a simple diet, and enjoying regular fresh air and exercise.

The King's Friends

Unfortunately, George's relations with Parliament were a lot more complicated than his family life. He disliked the way the Whigs had been allowed to dominate government since 1714, and was determined to take back some of the political power his predecessors had handed over to Parliament. A year after he came to the throne, George ousted Pitt and made Bute his Prime Minister. He also began replacing Whig politicians with his own supporters, known as the King's Friends. This didn't go down at all well in Parliament.

Regal deaths

Like his father before him, George II was always arguing with his son, Frederick, Prince of Wales. Prince Frederick spent much of his time gambling, playing sports and plotting against the King.

But he died before his father, of a brain haemorrhage, after being hit on the head with a cricket ball during a match.

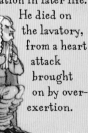

George II suffered from constipation in later life. He died on the lavatory, from a heart attack brought on by over-exertion.

Political pressure

The King faced savage criticism from a troublesome politician, John Wilkes. In his newspaper, *The North Briton*, Wilkes claimed that the King's interference was unconstitutional, and accused him of lying in Parliament. Wilkes was arrested, but soon set free again. Twice, he was expelled from Parliament, then voted back in again, under the slogan 'Wilkes and liberty'.

The unpopular Bute resigned after less than two years and four Prime Ministers came and went in quick succession. George struggled to trust them, and they were frustrated that the King continued to consult Bute behind their backs. In 1770, George finally found his man in Lord North, who would remain in office for a decade.

After Wilkes criticized William Hogarth's work, the artist produced this unflattering portrait of him as a cross-eyed, satanic figure.

This family portrait from 1770 shows George III and Queen Charlotte with six of their children. The future George IV is on the left in red, and the future William IV is in blue.

In this 1766 painting, *The Orrery* by Joseph Wright of Derby, a group gazes at a model of the Solar System while a scientist, in red, explains how it works.

"A wise man proportions his belief to the evidence."

Statements such as this earned the Scottish thinker, David Hume, criticism from religious leaders, who thought his theories contradicted their teachings.

The Age of Reason

As a boy, George III had been a slow learner, but as King, he was an enthusiastic patron of the arts and sciences, and an avid reader of all the latest ideas. He was fortunate to come to the throne at the height of an exciting period of scientific curiosity and discovery. It had begun during the 17th century, and was known as the Enlightenment, or the Age of Reason.

At its heart was an optimistic belief that by observing and exploring the world around them, and conducting experiments, scientists could shed new light on the mysteries of the universe. This theory was also applied to law, politics, economics and the arts, in the hope that all areas of human life could be improved by the powers of reason and common sense.

28

Scientific progress

British scientists made many new discoveries during the 18th century. Joseph Priestley, Joseph Black and Henry Cavendish identified the different chemicals that make up air and water. Humphrey Davy discovered that nitrous oxide – 'laughing gas' – could be used to put patients to sleep during surgery. He also invented a safety lamp for miners. In the field of medicine, William Smellie developed ways to make childbirth safer, and Edward Jenner introduced vaccination, to protect people against a deadly disease called smallpox.

In the know

Scientists formed societies, where they shared their latest findings, and they published them in pamphlets, newspapers and books. Many educated people were keen to stay informed. They read all the latest publications, invited guests to their homes to discuss the new ideas, attended public lectures and flocked to museums that were opening up around the country.

Collecting ideas

In 1753, a doctor named Sir Hans Sloane left his vast collection of books, manuscripts, natural history specimens and scientific instruments to the nation, on the condition that the government help to maintain it as a public museum – the British Museum.

Soon, other collectors, including George III, donated things to the museum's growing collection. The exhibits were classified and displayed according to their age, material or use. Often this helped to show a kind of progress from older, primitive forms to newer, more advanced examples.

From A to Z

Until the 18th century, there was no proper English dictionary, and there weren't any clear rules about English spellings or grammar.

So a journalist named Dr. Samuel Johnson began compiling a dictionary of the English language. After nine years' hard work, he finally finished this great task in 1755. Published in two massive volumes, the dictionary was 2,300 pages long, with over 42,000 entries.

In 1768 the first edition of the *Encyclopaedia Britannica* was published in Edinburgh. It aimed to be 'a dictionary of the Arts and Sciences' with articles arranged from A to Z by subject on all fields of knowledge. It was by far the largest, and most comprehensive encyclopaedia of its time.

Sailing the Pacific

In 1768, Captain James Cook, a navigator and explorer, set sail for the South Pacific on his ship, HMS *Endeavour*. He had two important missions. The first was to chart the transit of Venus over the Southern Ocean, near Tahiti. At that time, navigators relied on readings of the stars to calculate their position at sea. The Royal Navy hoped that these new readings would help British merchants to trade in new places.

Voyage of discovery

From Tahiti, Cook headed south, to carry out his second mission – to find and explore Australia, which had remained uncharted since Dutch sailors first reached its northern coast, in 1606. Cook was joined by a team of scientists whose task was to study the plants, wildlife, rocks and minerals in this new land. Among them was Joseph Banks, a young botanist (plant expert) who would later help George III set up the Royal Botanic Gardens at Kew.

John Harrison designed this 'chronometer' in 1759. It was the most accurate watch of its day, and a vital tool for navigators who needed to know the exact time to calculate their position at sea.

James Cook and his men raise the British flag at Botany Bay in Australia.

These paintings show two of the plants Joseph Banks collected. The plant on the left was called *Banksia*, after the botanist. On the right is a breadfruit.

After stopping at New Zealand on the way, Cook eventually arrived on the east coast of Australia in April 1770, and claimed the country for Britain. He later named the place where he landed Botany Bay, after its extraordinary range of strange, exotic plants.

Nearly three years after the voyage had begun, the *Endeavour* returned to England. Cook had charted over 8,000km (5,000 miles) of coastline; and Banks brought back detailed notes, drawings and samples of over 1,000 new plants and animals.

Settling down under

From the 1780s, British people began to settle in Australia. Many were criminals, who were sent there to work by the British government. But others were farmers looking for land. By the 1830s, there were about 100,000 Europeans living there. The native Australians, the Aboriginals, suffered terribly as a result. Many were forced off their land, or killed; others died of diseases brought by the newcomers.

All at sea

About half of sailors went to sea unwillingly. Not enough men volunteered for the navy, so captains sent out 'press gangs' to force any man who worked at sea to serve.

The diet on board was poor, vermin and diseases were a constant problem and discipline was harsh. Anyone not following orders could be punished with a lash, known as a cat-o-nine-tails.

George III attends an exhibition at the Royal Academy in Somerset House in London.

The art establishment

By the beginning of the 18th century, more people were buying art than ever before. Painters were constantly trying to think of new ways to advertise their work to these new buyers.

Like many other professional groups, artists had started to band together into societies. The main one was the Royal Academy, founded in 1768 with the support of George III. Under the guidance of its first president, Joshua Reynolds, the Academy hit upon a revolutionary way to meet the massive new demand for art – it put on large exhibitions. Art-lovers thronged to these displays, eager to buy or commission paintings, or just to absorb the atmosphere. But the Academy didn't only sell art. It had a huge influence over fashionable society, and was able to set trends too. Its works were seen to be the height of good taste, a reputation it maintained by carefully picking its members, and training young artists to work in its preferred styles.

This is a self-portrait by Joshua Reynolds, who was president of the Royal Academy from 1768 until his death in 1792.

32

Bands of musicians

Music was also hugely popular all across Georgian Britain. Small groups of music-lovers formed over the country, to perform concerts or just to enjoy singing simple tunes known as 'glees'. Meanwhile, larger music societies formed in the cities, culminating in the founding of the Royal Academy of Music, in 1822.

Club rules

The academies could be a mixed blessing. Their powerful influence meant that their views on style and taste held sway, and attempts to break away could be stifled. One artist who felt frustrated was Thomas Gainsborough, a member of the Royal Academy who was well-known for his portraits. He longed to earn a living from his less conventional landscape paintings instead, but failed to find any support. Eventually he left the Academy in disgust.

"Rule, Britannia! Britannia, rule the waves! Britons never, never, never shall be slaves!"

The words for the patriotic anthem *Rule Britannia!* were written by a Scottish poet named James Thompson, and set to music by the composer Thomas Arne, in 1740.

Mr. and Mrs. Andrews is a portrait of a fashionable landowner and his wife on their country estate. Thomas Gainsborough painted it in 1748-49.

Grand designs

As trade prospered and factories grew, merchants and factory owners across the country felt the benefits. Their growing incomes allowed them to live more luxuriously, and they became members of a new 'middle class'. Some even made fortunes to rival those of the established landed gentry.

As the newly wealthy urbanites thrived, they looked for houses to match their growing status. Even the richest businessmen who owned grand country estates still needed a base in the city to conduct their affairs.

From the 1760s, the rising demand for elegant town houses led to the renovation and growth of many cities, including Edinburgh, London and Bath. Many ports, such as Bristol and Liverpool, also expanded to become thriving cities based on trade.

This picture shows part of The Circus in Bath, designed by John Wood and completed by his son. It was the first circular street to be built in Britain, and its dimensions were based on measurements Wood had taken at Stonehenge.

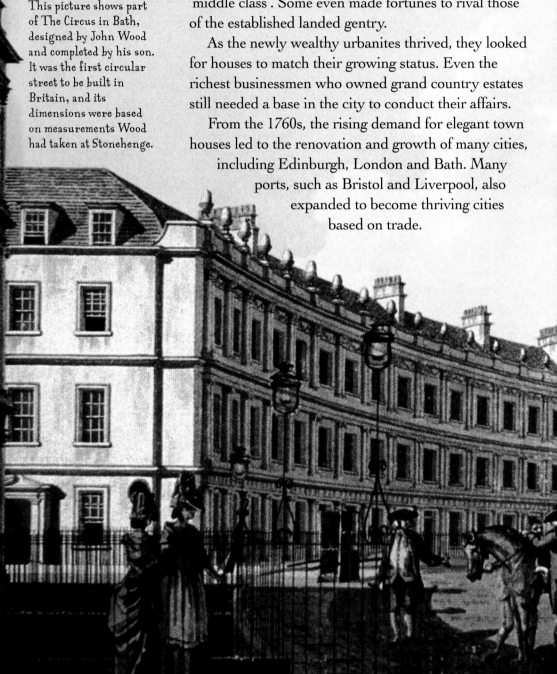

Urban planning

Georgian houses were designed to be regular and symmetrical, with clean lines and elegant facades. Tall and narrow, lots of these new houses were built side-by-side in long rows called terraces. As each house looked much like the next, for the first time, they were given numbers to tell them apart.

Many terraces sprang up as part of grand building projects. Carefully planned streets were laid out with curved crescents, squares, parks and wide streets designed for horse-drawn carriages. Whole sections of cities such as Edinburgh and Dublin were demolished to be rebuilt in this new style.

Famous architects

As more and more people were taking an interest in fashionable houses, many architects became household names. John Nash, Robert Adam and his brother James were celebrated for their work in London, and James Craig was the designer of much of the New Town in Edinburgh.

Windows and doors

Georgian houses had big windows, to let in lots of light. Nobody knew how to make large sheets of glass, so windows were made up of lots of little panes.

Doors were often flanked by classical-style pillars. They were topped with an intricate semi-circular window, called a fanlight.

Gorgeous interiors

Buying a town house was only the first step to becoming a respectable city dweller. The next task was to furnish the inside in the fashionable manner. Georgian ideas of taste and style were firmly fixed, and even a small slip could ruin the image of refined elegance.

Furniture fashions

The Georgian style of furniture was much like the architecture – graceful and refined. Georgian tables, chairs, sofas, cabinets and sideboards were made from expensive woods, and most had thin legs and simple shapes. Understated classical patterns were carved into the wood, or displayed on cushions and coverings. Later, other influences crept in too, particularly from eastern Asia. This style of furniture had a dark background overlaid with gold, often showing an 'oriental' scene.

Furniture was usually made by individual craftsmen. The most famous designers released books of their patterns, so they could be copied by other manufacturers across the country.

Wallpaper and rugs

The rest of the house had to match the fine furniture. Fireplaces, doorways and even ceilings were richly carved. Floors were covered with oriental rugs, and walls were painted or decorated with wallpaper, which was the very latest fashion.

Objects of desire

The richest families filled their homes with stylish items, made by the very best craftsmen.

This mahogany chair was created by Thomas Chippendale, one of the best-known Georgian designers.

Josiah Wedgwood owned a big factory where he produced pottery in a classical style.

This piece was based on a famous Roman vase, which showed scenes from ancient myths.

Items imported from Asia were very popular, such as this tea set from China. Sets like this were used by rich families to serve tea, which had become the height of fashion.

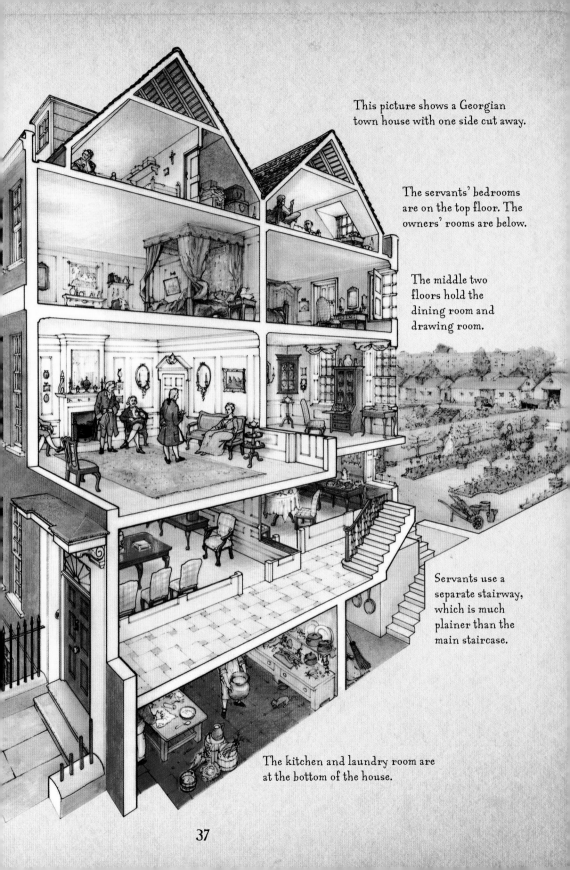

This picture shows a Georgian town house with one side cut away.

The servants' bedrooms are on the top floor. The owners' rooms are below.

The middle two floors hold the dining room and drawing room.

Servants use a separate stairway, which is much plainer than the main staircase.

The kitchen and laundry room are at the bottom of the house.

Poverty and principle

While the middle classes enjoyed the wealth and the luxury goods that the new industries brought, these came at a price. Most of the workers that kept the industries going had been forced to move to towns and cities, where they lived in over-crowded, filthy slums, on very low wages. Their plight mostly went unheeded, but some well-to-do citizens worked tirelessly to help them, often motivated by religious beliefs.

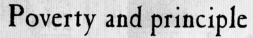

John Wesley gave over 40,000 outdoor services in industrial towns up and down the country. Poor workers made up most of his audiences.

A broad church

Migrants to the cities often stopped going to church. They lost their old ties to the Church, or found that busy urban churches had no space left, and many people thought that the Church wasn't doing enough to help them. So a preacher named John Wesley decided to take religion to the workers. He rode around the country giving open-air sermons, and later built churches where there weren't enough. Wesley and his followers became known as Methodists, and many were involved in charity work and social reform.

This picture shows the chapel of Coram's Foundling Hospital, where charity performances of Handel's *Messiah* were given regularly.

Sunday schools

There was no compulsory education in the 18th century, and most schooling cost money. Children from poor families worked long hours at paid jobs, so could spare neither the time nor the money for education. Appalled by conditions in the towns around her Somerset home, one writer named Hannah More set up a string of free Sunday schools, where local children received religious instruction and learned to read.

Saving the children

On his return to London, a sea captain named Thomas Coram was shocked by the sight of children living on the streets. Many were orphans, or had been abandoned by parents who couldn't afford to look after them. Coram set up a 'Foundling Hospital' for homeless children, and famous artists and musicians gave their support.

Reformers such as Wesley, More and Coram could only help a small number of those in need. Many of the poorest people had little power to improve their lives. If they couldn't pay their bills, they were sent to prison – and had to pay fees to wardens while they were there. Others starved on the streets.

Behind bars

To help the women and children in Newgate Prison, Elizabeth Fry set up a school and provided inmates with items so that they could knit and sew goods to sell.

She also made sure that the prisoners were given regular Bible readings.

Breaking the chains

"I have seen a negro beaten till some of his bones were broken, for only letting a pot boil over."

Eduiano describes the cruel punishment of a slave in the Caribbean.

This picture shows slaves working on a plantation. They are taking sugar cane to a windmill to crush out the juice so it can be refined to make sugar.

The buying and selling of people as slaves had been going on since ancient times. But, by the 18th century, this trade had increased dramatically, generating great wealth for European merchants – and causing terrible suffering for the slaves. During the 1720s, British ships sailing from London, Bristol and Liverpool transported some 200,000 Africans to North America and the Caribbean. By the 1790s, that number had doubled.

Those who survived the dreadful voyage were then sold to work on plantations where they were made to work long hours, and often beaten. Many slaves tried to escape or rebel against their masters. A few were successful, but many were punished brutally.

As people in Britain began to hear of the harsh realities of slavery, some began to demand an end to the trade. They met opposition at first, but eventually slavery was abolished in Britain and throughout its colonies.

1760

A slave named Tacky leads a massive rebellion in Jamaica. Sugar crops are set alight and around 60 white people are killed. Tacky and 400 other rebels die or are executed.

~

Quaker leaders ban their followers from slave trading.

June, 1772

James Somerset, a slave, escapes from his owner in London. His case is taken to court, and he is declared a free man. Many people mistakenly take this to mean that slavery is now outlawed in England.

1774

Methodist preacher John Wesley publishes an anti-slavery pamphlet entitled *Thoughts upon Slavery.*

1787

Granville Sharp and Thomas Clarkson found the Society for the Abolition of the Slave Trade. They persuade MP William Wilberforce to be their spokesman in Parliament.

November 1781

The captain of a slave ship, *Zong* throws 133 slaves overboard alive, then files an insurance claim for their value. The case shocks many people into joining the fight against slavery.

1787

Josiah Wedgwood produces the Abolition Society's seal. It includes the motto, "Am I Not a Man and a Brother?"

1789

A former slave named Olaudah Equiano publishes his autobiography. It becomes a bestseller.

1792

Freetown, in Sierra Leone, west Africa, is established under British rule as a home for former slaves.

1789

Wilberforce makes his first anti-slavery speech to the House of Commons.

1807

The slave trade is abolished in Britain and its empire, but slave ownership continues in British colonies.

1831

A slave named Sam Sharpe leads a rebellion of over 2,000 slaves in Jamaica. British troops restore order, but the rebellion inspires people in Britain to renew the fight against slavery.

1833

Slavery is abolished in all British colonies.

The American Revolution

By the 1770s, many people in Britain's American colonies had become resentful of British rule. King George III's government enforced strict controls on trade to and from the colonies, and imposed increasingly heavy taxes on them, too. The colonists felt this was unfair. As they didn't have representatives in Parliament in London, they thought they should only pay taxes approved by their own governing assemblies. Many began to protest more and more vehemently against British rule, and some of these protests led to violence.

Storm in a teacup

One of the most infamous anti-tax protests took place in 1773, after the British refused to remove import tax on tea.

Some colonists stopped buying tea in protest, but a party of men in Boston took things further. Disguised as Native Americans, they stormed a ship bringing tea into the port and threw its cargo overboard.

This protest became known as the Boston Tea Party.

Congress signs the Declaration of Independence, July 4, 1776.

A united stand

In May 1775, representatives from 13 of the colonies met at the Congress of Philadelphia. They decided it was time to break away from British rule. So, they set up an army under the command of a soldier named George Washington. On July 4, 1776, Congress signed a document called the Declaration of Independence. This stated that the colonies were now an independent country – the United States of America.

42

Losing America

The British weren't going to give up without a fight. Their army was stronger and better trained than Washington's troops, and won several early battles. But, as the American troops grew tougher and more experienced, they became more successful. They also gained allies in the French, the Spanish and the Dutch, who saw the war as a chance to weaken British influence in America.

In 1781, after a fierce fight at the Battle of Yorktown, the war finally ended in victory for the colonies. Two years later, at the Treaty of Paris, Britain officially recognized the United States of America as an independent nation. In Britain, many people held George III to blame for losing America, and his Prime Minister Lord North was forced to resign.

Washington

The leaders of the United States soon began to build the foundations of their new country.

In 1789, George Washington was elected the first President of the USA.

His government, and all future US governments, followed the American Constitution, a set of laws written by a lawyer named Thomas Jefferson.

In this scene, British soldiers are defending their position from a makeshift wooden fort.

The Americans are fighting under their new flag. It has 13 stripes, one for each of the colonies.

Heads roll

In 1792, the French abolished their monarchy. The following year, they beheaded their royal family using a machine known as a guillotine.

This horrified many people in Britain, not least Queen Charlotte, who feared the same thing might happen in Britain.

The rights of man

After losing America, George III faced a difficult time with his ministers – until 1783, when he found a talented and supportive politician to lead his government. William Pitt the Younger – the 24-year-old son of William Pitt who had held power during the Seven Years' War – would be Prime Minister from 1783-1801, and 1804-6, steering the nation through a series of events that threatened to topple the King and his government.

The first of these came in November 1788, when the King suffered what his doctors described as a fit of insanity. He began talking gibberish and foaming at the mouth. His eyes became so bloodshot that one observer said they looked like currant jelly. The episode was short-lived, and by April 1789, George had returned to his royal duties. But a far more serious threat lay ahead.

Reason and republicanism

The Americans weren't the only people with revolutionary ideas. In France, writers Voltaire and Jean Jacques Rousseau had begun to apply Enlightenment principles to society, claiming that all people were equal and that the idea of a monarchy was irrational and outmoded.

An English writer, Thomas Paine, held similar views, and had taken part in the American Revolution. He published a pamphlet, entitled *Common Sense*, which argued for republicanism – government by the people, with an elected head of state instead of a monarch.

This cartoon, by James Gillray, depicts Thomas Paine as a dangerous man, spreading nonsense, anarchy and misery.

Revolution in France

In the summer of 1789, ideas were put into action as revolution broke out in France. At first, the French ruler, Louis XVI, was made to sign a new constitution that gave him only limited powers in government. But in 1792, the French abolished the monarchy altogether and declared their country a republic.

Thomas Paine celebrated the French Revolution in his pamphlet, *Rights of Man*. It became a bestseller, as many in Britain greeted the news from France with similar enthusiasm. But this turned to outrage and alarm in 1793, when the French royal family and hundreds of 'enemies of the revolution' were executed during a period known as the Reign of Terror.

Just as Pitt was debating how to react to the threat from across the Channel, the French declared war.

In this painting from 1793, Pitt the Younger stands in the House of Commons to announce the French declaration of war.

To prevent revolution breaking out in Britain, Pitt brought in emergency powers. Anyone who might pose a threat to national security was arrested. Thomas Paine escaped to France, but many political campaigners were imprisoned.

Rebellion in Ireland

This is a picture of the leading members of the United Irishmen.

Standing in the middle, hat in hand, is Robert Emmet. He was a young leader of the United Irishmen, who survived the 1798 rebellion by fleeing to France. He was later caught and executed for treason.

Two people to the right of Emmet, standing by the pillar, is Theobald Wolfe Tone. Tone was a Protestant lawyer who was deeply committed to improving the rights of Catholics.

Since the Battle of the Boyne in 1690, most of the land in Ireland had been owned by Protestants with close ties to Britain. Meanwhile, Ireland's Catholic majority had very limited rights. They couldn't vote, own land, educate their children or become politicians or lawyers.

Ireland had its own Parliament, but its decisions were highly influenced by the British government. Members of the Irish Parliament were coerced or bribed into voting the way that Britain wanted.

Demanding change

In 1791, a group of Catholics and Protestants joined to form the United Irishmen. Inspired by the American and French revolutions, they aimed to break away from Britain and form their own republic, with better rights for Catholics. One of the leaders, Theobald Wolfe Tone, went to ask the French for military support.

Revolution and reaction

In the spring of 1798, the United Irishmen launched an
uprising. The French sent troops but they didn't arrive
in time to help, and British forces were able to crush
the rebellion at the Battle of Vinegar Hill in June.

Meanwhile, French troops landed in Mayo, on the
west coast. But, despite a summer victory at Castlebar,
they were also soon forced to surrender. Tone landed in
Donegal with further French forces, but was captured
by the British and committed suicide in prison.

A new kingdom

To prevent more uprisings, the British government
decided to tighten its grip on Ireland. Pitt the Younger
persuaded the Irish Parliament to disband. In return,
he offered better rights for Catholics, and allowed Irish
representatives to sit in Britain's Parliament in London.

In 1801, the Act of Union joined Ireland and
Britain to form the new United Kingdom. But
George III, who was a staunch Protestant,
refused to pass the law giving
Catholics their promised rights.
Ashamed that he couldn't keep
his word, Pitt resigned.

1606 flag

Irish flag

Union
flag

The Union flag

In 1606, King James IV
of Scotland and I of
England had a new
British flag made. It
combined the flags of the
two nations he ruled.

In 1801 the Irish flag was
added – to create the
British flag that is still
used today.

Ireland in 1798

This map shows where the key
battles and uprisings took place.

✗ Battle

✗ United Irish uprising

▨ Area of United Irish activity

▨ Area occupied by the French

ULSTER

DONEGAL

Antrim

Belfast ●

Ballynahinch

Killala ●

● Sligo

MAYO

CONNACHT

Castlebar

Ballynamuck

Tara

LEINSTER

● Dublin

The Curragh

● Wicklow

Arklow

Gorey

MUNSTER

Vinegar Hill

New Ross

● Wexford

Cork ●

Bantry

Napoleon and Nelson

The French failed to take the revolution to Ireland, but by 1797, they had defeated much of Europe. Much of their success was down to the skills of a charismatic general, named Napoleon Bonaparte, who was rapidly rising through the ranks.

Napoleon seemed unbeatable, but at sea he met his match in the British naval commander, Horatio Nelson. Nelson was convinced that the mighty Royal Navy could save the country and change the course of the war. In August 1798, his fleet destroyed the French navy in the Mediterranean, at the Battle of the Nile. From then on, he enjoyed a series of victories at sea.

By the turn of the century, Napoleon was effectively ruling France as a military dictator. There was a brief period of peace, but fighting broke out again in 1802.

Napoleon's rise to power

1769 – born in Corsica.

1782 – attends military school in Paris.

1793 – helps lead a siege at the French port of Toulon to defeat anti-revolutionary forces.

1796 – marries Josephine de Beauharnais, commands the French army in Italy, and forces Austria to make peace with France.

1798 – conquers Egypt in order to block British trade routes to India. He is later defeated by Nelson's navy at the Battle of the Nile.

1799 – disbands the French government, the Directory, and appoints himself First Consul – he is effectively a military dictator.

1804 – crowns himself Emperor Napoleon I.

This painting of the Battle of Trafalgar shows a fight between a French warship, on the left, and a British one, as they fire their cannons at each other.

Trafalgar

In 1803, Napoleon started gathering an army to invade Britain. But his soldiers couldn't cross the English Channel without naval support, and Nelson was determined that they would never get that far.

On October 21, 1805, Nelson's fleet met a combined French and Spanish force off Cape Trafalgar, near the southern tip of Spain. Using his three most powerful warships "like a spear to break the enemy line," Nelson sent the rival fleet scattering. In the hard-fought battle that followed, Nelson was shot and later died. But his tactic had paid off, and the superior skills and experience of Britain's seamen won the day.

Nelson's victory at Trafalgar removed the immediate threat of invasion, and encouraged other countries to stand up to France – but Napoleon wasn't beaten yet.

Nelson's column

Nelson served in the navy from the age of 12. He lost his right arm and the sight in his right eye in earlier battles, but was mortally wounded at Trafalgar. On hearing that the British were winning, his dying words were, "Thank God I have done my duty."

Nelson was immortalized with a giant 5.5m (18ft) statue of him, erected at the top of a 46m (150ft) high column. Nelson's Column, as the landmark is called, towers over Trafalgar Square in the heart of London.

Wellington and Waterloo

Suited and booted

Wellington had his shoemaker modify his boots so that they were sturdy and comfortable in battle, but smart enough for evenings.

'Wellington boots' soon became the latest fashion among soldiers and dandies alike, but it wasn't until the 1850s that the first rubber 'wellies' were manufactured.

Wellington raises his hat aloft as a signal to his troops to advance, in this artist's impression of the Battle of Waterloo.

By 1812, Napoleon had conquered most of western Europe. But his days in power were numbered, as Britain and many European countries formed a new alliance to beat him once and for all.

In June that year, he led a disastrous invasion of Russia. Badly equipped and ill-prepared for the harsh winter, of 600,000 men, only about 30,000 returned. Meanwhile, a British army, led by Arthur Wellesley, later the Duke of Wellington, helped to drive out the French from Spain and Portugal. These losses marked a turning point in Napoleon's fortunes. After several major defeats, he was captured in April 1814, and imprisoned on the Italian island of Elba.

The Hundred Days

A year later, Napoleon escaped and retook power in France for a brief period, known as the Hundred Days. In June, he led his armies to Belgium to face his enemies in what was to be the final, decisive battle at Waterloo.

Into battle

Two forces were assembled in Belgium, ready to do battle with Napoleon: an army of 89,000 men from the German state of Prussia, led by a veteran fighter, Field Marshal Blücher, and an allied force of 68,000 British, Dutch, German and Belgian soldiers under Wellington.

Napoleon's strategy was to launch lightning attacks on his opponents, before the two armies could join forces and outnumber his 71,000 troops. On June 16, he struck the Prussians at Ligny, forcing them to retreat. Thinking Blücher was defeated, Napoleon turned his attentions to Wellington on June 18, 1815.

A close-run thing

Wellington's men held a defensive position on a ridge of land, just south of Waterloo. At midday, the French opened fire, with a massive artillery barrage. Wellington ordered his men to stand firm. His foot soldiers formed tight squares behind the ridge, while his gunmen fired at Napoleon's advancing troops. There were heavy losses on both sides, but the French failed to break through the allied line.

Just as daylight was beginning to fade, the Prussians arrived, and the combined allied forces charged their opponents. The French were routed, and fled back to Paris. As the smoke from the cannons lifted, 25,000 French and 22,000 allied soldiers lay dead or wounded. Wellington later described the battle as "the closest-run thing you ever saw in your life."

His empire in tatters, Napoleon finally surrendered to the British in July. His defeat ended French domination of Europe for good.

Island exile

After his defeat at Waterloo, Napoleon was sent to live in exile on the tiny, remote island of St. Helena in the South Atlantic Ocean.

Thousands of miles from anywhere, with no means of escape, Napoleon died on the island on May 5, 1821. His doctor claimed he died of stomach cancer, but some historians believe he might have died as a result of arsenic poisoning.

This cartoon shows Napoleon in his earlier island exile, on Elba.

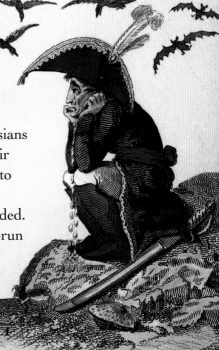

Mad, bad and dangerous

While the Napoleonic Wars were raging, an artistic movement, known as Romanticism, swept across Europe too. Partly inspired by revolutionary politics, and partly reacting against ideas of the Enlightenment, Romantic poets, painters and composers began to explore new styles and new sources of inspiration.

Radical politics

One of the first English Romantics was William Blake. He studied at the Royal Academy, then worked as a printer and engraver, publishing his own poems, which he also illustrated himself. A supporter of Thomas Paine and the revolutions in America and France, many of his poems expressed his passionate beliefs in social equality and creative freedom.

As an idealistic young man, the poet William Wordsworth spent time in France during the early days of the French Revolution. He lost faith in the revolution and returned to England in 1793, as the fight for equality and liberty turned to terror and bloodshed.

Wild genius

In 1798, Wordsworth and another poet, Samuel Taylor Coleridge, brought out a collection of their poems entitled *Lyrical Ballads*. In it, they set out a revolutionary manifesto for poetry. Imagination and emotions were more important to them than reason and order. They wanted to move away from the formal styles of previous generations, to write the way they spoke. A Scottish poet, Robert Burns, took this even further by writing many poems in his own local dialect.

Along with painters such as J.M.W. Turner and John Constable, many Romantic poets were inspired by nature and Britain's wild landscapes. For them, dramatic scenes of mountains, lakes and coastlines stirred powerful feelings, which they expressed in their work.

Some poets, particularly Lord Byron, Percy Shelley and John Keats, took their pursuit of sensations to extremes. They became notorious not only for their literary talents, but also for their wild antics. The rock stars of their day, they all died young.

Gothic horror

In 1816, Byron invited Percy Shelley and Shelley's future wife Mary to stay with him near Lake Geneva in the Swiss Alps. It was a cold, wet summer, so they spent much of their time huddled indoors, and set themselves a challenge to see who could write the most frightening story.

Mary, aged only 19, wrote *Frankenstein*, a tale of a young medical student who builds a man from parts of dead bodies and then brings this monster to life.

Byron wrote only part of a vampire story. But this later led another guest, John Polidori, to write *The Vampyre*. His vampire character was based on Byron, and inspired Bram Stoker to create Count Dracula.

Regency style

This illustration shows stylish Georgians strolling in Brighton, with the Royal Pavilion in the background. The Prince Regent lived in Brighton until his father's death, and under his influence the town was transformed from a small seaside town to a fashionable resort.

Brighton Royal Pavilion was designed by John Nash for the Prince Regent. Its exotic facade was inspired by the Prince's love of Indian and oriental architecture.

In 1811, George III suffered another attack of the illness that had first struck him in 1788. Many experts now believe his symptoms were caused by a rare condition called porphyria. But at the time, the King's doctors believed he was insane. They subjected him to a series of humiliating treatments, including being force-fed and restrained in an iron chair.

Despite his doctors' efforts, the King never fully recovered. So, his son George became Prince Regent, ruling on behalf of his father. The regency period would last until the death of George III, in 1820.

The Prince Regent was a completely different character from his father. Intelligent, handsome and sociable, he was admired as a man of style with refined artistic tastes. But he also had extravagant tastes for heavy drinking, excessive eating and reckless gambling.

Out and about

In many ways, the Prince Regent set the trends for Britain's well-to-do. Balls, parties and lavish dinners were commonplace across the country, and even small towns had Assembly Rooms for public dances. Other popular pastimes included gambling at cards and horse races, and attending plays and concerts in the cities.

But there was also a serious purpose to much of this socializing. Being seen to be fashionable and rich was vital for making business contacts, and for young adults looking to marry someone from a respectable family.

Taking the waters

Another popular pastime was making trips to coastal or spa towns, to bathe in the water. Visitors flocked to stylish resorts such as Bath, Cheltenham and Brighton, the Prince Regent's own regular haunt. These towns were designed largely for pleasure, with rows of trees, romantic gardens, and many evening entertainments.

Witty writer

Jane Austen wrote six novels, set among the upper and middle classes of Regency society. The stories make witty observations of the manners and customs of the time, and give an insight into women's lives in particular. The Prince Regent was said to admire her books, which are still widely read today.

Greek goddesses and dashing dandies

During the Regency period, fashions moved away from the powdered wigs, frills and embroidery of the 18th century, and became simpler and more sophisticated.

Instead of having tight bodices and full skirts, women began to wear 'empire line' dresses. These had high waists and loose, flowing skirts draped to look like the dresses of Greek statues.

Fashionable young men, or 'dandies' were influenced by the Prince Regent's friend George 'Beau' Brummell. They wore long breeches or trousers, tailored waistcoats, crisp linen shirts with cravats, and they didn't wear wigs.

Paper or silk parasols shaded women's fair skin from the sun.

Both women and men used fans to keep cool, and also for flirting at parties.

Coal, iron and rocket power

By the end of the 18th century, Britain's factories had found a new source of power: steam.

The very first steam engine had been built back in 1698 by an English engineer named Thomas Savery. It drove a pump to drain flooded coal mines. The engine broke down frequently, so a few years later, Thomas Newcomen improved on the design, making it more reliable.

Watt's engine

Then, around 1764, James Watt, a Scottish engineer, was given a Newcomen engine to repair. He spent the next few years developing more efficient engines that had the power to run whole factories. By 1800 there were over 500 of Watt's engines in Britain's mines, ironworks, mills and factories and he retired, a wealthy man. A unit of power – the Watt – is named after him.

Spanning the River Severn, in Shropshire this is the world's first iron bridge, built by Abraham Darby at Coalbrookdale in 1779.

Darby's grandfather, also named Abraham Darby, set up an ironworks at Coalbrookdale in 1709. He developed a process of producing iron goods on a much bigger scale than had been possible before.

As most steam engines and industrial machines were made from iron, Darby's work played a crucial role in the Industrial Revolution.

Locomotives

Soon, a mining engineer named Richard Trevithick realized that steam engines could replace horses for driving heavy vehicles. In 1804, he produced the first steam-powered train, or locomotive, to run on rails.

Trevithick's ideas were taken further by George Stephenson. He improved the designs of both locomotives and the rails they ran on. In 1825, he built the world's first public steam railway, which ran 40km (25 miles) from Stockton to Darlington. He also designed the engine that carried coal trucks and passenger wagons along the line.

With the help of these engines, and plentiful supplies of coal to fuel them, the railways expanded all over the country during the 19th century, and the Industrial Revolution rapidly gathered pace.

This is a sketch of one of Richard Trevithick's designs for a steam engine. His inventions helped many engineers after him, but didn't make him much money. Sadly, he died a pauper.

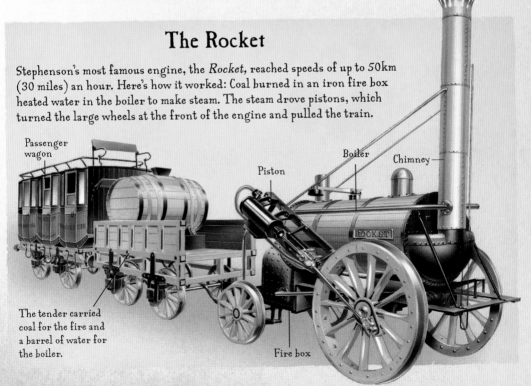

The Rocket

Stephenson's most famous engine, the *Rocket*, reached speeds of up to 50km (30 miles) an hour. Here's how it worked: Coal burned in an iron fire box heated water in the boiler to make steam. The steam drove pistons, which turned the large wheels at the front of the engine and pulled the train.

Passenger wagon

Piston

Boiler

Chimney

The tender carried coal for the fire and a barrel of water for the boiler.

Fire box

This cartoon shows the chaos and carnage of the Peterloo Massacre. The cavalry soldier on the left is saying, "chop 'em down my brave boys... the more you kill the less poor rates you'll have to pay."

Fancy dress

After ruling Britain for nearly nine years, the Prince Regent became King George IV in 1820. Despite the poverty of many of his subjects, he spent thousands of pounds on a lavish Tudor-style coronation.

Riots and reforms

While socialites lived it up, the gap between the lives of the rich and the poor was growing. Mostly, only rich landowners were allowed to vote in elections, so the needs of poor people, and even the middle classes, were often ignored in Parliament. The first decades of the 19th century saw much unrest, as many people began protesting against inequality and demanding change.

Since the outbreak of the French Revolution, it had been illegal for British workers to join trades unions. This meant they couldn't negotiate with their employers for better pay or conditions. In desperation, some took matters into their own hands.

In 1811, a group of stocking weavers in Nottingham began smashing up factory machinery that was putting them out of work. They became known as Luddites after their leader, Ned Ludd. Similar protests took place throughout the north of England.

58

Give us bread

During the war with France, wages had been frozen, but the price of many goods had tripled. A series of bad harvests led to a shortage of grain, and an even steeper rise in the price of bread. The answer was to import grain to keep bread cheap, but many landowners thought this would harm British farming. So in 1815, the government passed the Corn Law, banning the importing of cheap grain. Unable to afford the food they needed to survive, the hungry masses took to the streets.

In August 1819, tens of thousands of men, women and children gathered for a peaceful demonstration in St. Peter's Fields, in Manchester. Local magistrates feared the gathering could turn into a riot, so they sent in cavalry soldiers to arrest its leaders. They rode into the crowd with their swords drawn, causing mayhem: 11 people were killed and 400 were injured. Some of the soldiers had fought at Waterloo, so this tragic event was given the ironic nickname the 'Peterloo Massacre'.

Small steps and giant leaps

Under increasing pressure from protesters and reformers, the government began to take steps to make life easier for poor people. Gradually, new laws brought better working conditions in factories and improved the state of Britain's prisons.

The call for political reforms was growing louder too, but the ruling classes were reluctant to lose their grip on power. Not only were few people allowed to vote, but many of the new industrial towns had no Member of Parliament to represent them. Meanwhile, some MPs stood for areas, known as 'rotten boroughs', where only a handful of electors lived. Something had to change.

Getting better

Here are some of the key social reforms of the early 19th century:

1823 – The death penalty is removed from over a hundred crimes. Conditions in prisons are improved and wages for jailers are introduced.

1824 – The ban on trade union membership is lifted.

1829 – The Roman Catholic Relief Act allows Catholics to sit in Parliament. They had been given the vote in 1793.

1829 – The Metropolitan Police is set up in London.

1832 – The Great Reform Act improves the electoral system and gives more men the vote.

1833 – Factory Acts make it illegal to employ children under 9 in factories, and limits the hours children under 13 can be made to work.

The sailor and the actress

Before he became King, William had served in the Royal Navy for 47 years.

In 1789, he was made Duke of Clarence. He retired from the Navy a year later, and lived with his mistress, an actress named Dorothea Jordan.

Their children, known as the Fitzclarences, weren't seen as heirs to the throne as the couple weren't married.

Time for change

With the coming of the age of steam, and social reforms under way, there was a general sense that Britain was on the brink of a new era. This was reinforced in 1830, when George IV died, and his 64-year-old brother succeeded him as William IV. But a more significant change came later that year. The Tories, who had dominated government for decades, were voted out and a Whig, Earl Grey, became Prime Minister.

To prevent the revolution they feared was brewing, the Whigs set about bringing in electoral reforms Despite strong opposition, the Great Reform Act was passed in 1832. The vote was extended to more people, and rotten boroughs were abolished. The vast majority of the population still wasn't allowed to vote, but the act was a major landmark on the road to a more democratic government.

A new order

In October 1834, a fire ravaged the Palace of Westminster, the ancient seat of the Houses of Parliament and a powerful symbol of the old order. The fire was an accident, but many commentators believed this was just the fresh start the reformed Parliament needed, and the government launched a competition to design a new building.

On June 20, 1837, William IV died. His brother, Ernest Augustus, Duke of Cumberland, became Elector of Hanover, and his 18-year-old niece, Victoria, succeeded him to the British throne. With industry booming and a bright young monarch, the difficulties of the early 19th century seemed to be over. Many people looked forward to a better future.

Mother's pride

Princess Victoria turned 18 only a month before King William died. If he had died earlier, Victoria's mother, the ambitious Duchess of Kent – who William greatly disliked – would have taken over until Victoria was old enough to rule by herself.

People watch from boats on the Thames as the old Houses of Parliament are consumed in flames, in this painting by a Scottish artist, David Roberts.

Index

Acknowledgements

Every effort has been made to trace and acknowledge ownership of copyright. If any rights have been omitted, the publishers offer to rectify this in any future editions following notification. The publishers are grateful to the following individuals and organizations for their permission to reproduce material on the following pages: (t=top, b=bottom, l=left, r=right)

cover (tl) Private Collection/Bridgeman, **(tr)** Brighton Pavillion/The Art Archive, **(b)** © Historical Picture Archive/CORBIS.

p1 Cliveden House, Buckinghamshire, UK/ Bridgeman; **p2-3** © Victoria Art Gallery, Bath and North East Somerset Council/Bridgeman; **p6** © Bettman/Corbis; **p8 (b)** British Museum, London, UK/Bridgeman; **p9 (br)** Courtesy of the Council, National Army Museum, London, UK, Acquired with assistance of National Art Collections Fund/Bridgeman; **p10 (t)** © Robert Harding Picture Library Ltd/Alamy; **p11 (bl)** © V&A Images/Alamy, **(br)** National Trust Photographic Library/John Hammond/Bridgeman; **p12 (b)** The Art Archive/Eileen Tweedy; **p13 (tl)** © Burstein Collection/Corbis; **p14** © The Drambuie Collection, Edinburgh, Scotland/Bridgeman; **p15 (t)** The Art Archive/Eileen Tweedy; **p17** The Art Archive/Eileen Tweedy; **p18 (l)** © Louie Psihoyos/Corbis; **p19 (t)** The Art Archive/General Wolfe Museum Quebec House/Eileen Tweedy; **p21** © National Portrait Gallery, London; **p22 (tl)** Science Museum/SSPL; **p22-23** Science Museum, London, UK/Bridgeman; **p24** The Art Archive/British Museum/Eileen Tweedy; **p25 (t)** Science Museum/SSPL; **p27 (tr)** © Michael Nicholson/Corbis, **(b)** The Royal Collection © 2008, Her Majesty Queen Elizabeth II; **p28 (t)** © The Gallery Collection/Corbis; **p30 (tl)** Science Museum/ SSPL, **(b)** The Art Archive/Royal Commonwealth Society/Eileen Tweedy; **p31 (tl)** Alecto Historical Editions, London, UK/Bridgeman, **(tr)** © National Library of Australia, Canberra, Australia/Bridgeman; **p32 (t)** Private Collection/Bridgeman, **(b)** © Photo Scala Florence, Uffizi Gallery 1990; **p33 (b)** Thomas Gainsborough, Mr and Mrs Andrews © The National Gallery, London; **p34-35** The Art Archive/Victoria Art Gallery Bath; **p36-37** © John Ronayne/Geffrye Museum; **p38-39** The Art Archive/Private Collection/ Eileen Tweedy; **p40-41** © British Library Board. All Rights Reserved/Bridgeman; **p42** © Hulton Archive/ Getty Images; **p43 (tr)** © Philadelphia Museum of Art/Corbis; **p44 (bl)** British Museum, London, UK/ Bridgeman; **p45 (t)** National Portrait Gallery, London, UK/Bridgeman; **p46 (t)** Private Collection/ Bridgeman; **p48 (tl)** © Archivo Iconografico, S.A./Corbis; **p48-49** © The Gallery Collection/Corbis; **p50 (cl)** The Art Archive/ Wellington Museum London/Eileen Tweedy, **(b)** The Art Archive/British Museum; **p51 (br)** The Art Archive/ Wellington Museum London/Eileen Tweedy; **p52 (tl)** Mary Evans; **p52-53** The Art Archive/Victoria and Albert Museum London/Sally Chappell; **p54 (t)** Mary Evans; **p55 (tr)** © Topfoto; **p56 (t)** © Rob Reichenfeld/Dorling Kindersley/Getty Images; **p57 (tr)** © National Railway Museum/SSPL; **p58 (t)** © Mary Evans Picture Library/Alamy; **p60-61** Houses of Parliament, Westminster, London, UK/Bridgeman; **p61 (tr)** Mary Evans.

Additional design by Brenda Cole, & Steve Wood
Additional illustration by Dai Evans
Digital design by John Russell; Picture research by Ruth King